Erotic Foods

Erotic Foods

◆

grape goddess® guides to good living

Advice decadently laced with juicy insider tips, anecdotes, and real-life experience from a world-renowned Master Sommelier, bon vivant, and lover of luxury in all its forms.

by Catherine Fallis, Master Sommelier

iUniverse, Inc.

New York Lincoln Shanghai

Erotic Foods
grape goddess® guides to good living

All Rights Reserved © 2004 by Catherine Fallis

iUniverse, Inc.

For information address:
iUniverse, Inc.
2021 Pine Lake Road, Suite 100
Lincoln, NE 68512
www.iuniverse.com

ISBN: 0-595-32698-6

Printed in the United States of America

Thank you to my Nana, the late Lucille Leone Kendall, who provided unending love and nourishment for my body and soul when no one else would. She was my rock.

Thank you to my Nana, too, for teaching me to chew with my mouth shut, thus making me aware of manners and etiquette for the first time. Her spirit lives on in me.

Thank you to my soul mate and baby brother, the late Sidney Fallis, a constant source of inspiration to me. He was an artist in so many senses of the word, an entrepreneur, and an amazing Dad. His spirit lives on in his sons, my nephews, who constantly amaze me with the same joyful song, dance, and clowning around that filled the house when he was alive.

Thank you to my sister-in-law and her husband for providing such a loving home to the boys.

Thank you to my brother Christopher Kendall Fallis and his wife for providing love, support, general advice, and life lessons on being a foster parent. Thank you to their children, my niece and nephew, for giving me renewed appreciation for the single life.

Thank you to my brother Alex for cheering me on and providing unending witty commentary.

Thank you to my brother James for showing such strength of character. Thank you to my sister, Christina, for having the courage to take the plunge into the culinary world.

To Kevin Zraly, I thank you from the bottom of my heart for believing in me.

Writing is a solitary activity requiring great concentration. To my neglected friends and family members, I thank you for your understanding and patience.

Contents

Preface

Embracing the Senses

Sensual pleasures—pleasures of sight, of sound, of smell, of taste, and of feeling—are what this guide is all about. Aphrodisiacs are sensual pleasures that stimulate or intensify sexual desire.

Sex is a popular topic. We think about it, read about it, talk about it, hear about it, and want more of it, but as an on-the-go society, we hardly ever take the time to actually have it! I've created this guide for people like you, who would like to rekindle a flame or to fan the fires of a new relationship but who may be just too exhausted at the end of the day to do anything but crawl into bed with a pint of ice cream.

Making love is as natural an act as eating. As creatures of nature, we are percolating with sensual, and sexual, energy. We are programmed to share our energy with other creatures. Touching, hugging, caressing, and kissing are energy exchanges. We feel good giving and receiving. When sparks fly, the energy becomes sexual. Tapping into these primal urges and seeking sensual pleasures is okay. Have no guilt! Simply slow down, sit back, relax, and enjoy the ride.

For easy reference I've organized this guide by type of aphrodisiac. For hunting and gathering, I've included a shopping guide in chapter III, with products and services that grape goddess recommends. To make the cut, they must be of outstanding quality, be fairly priced, and be generally available. For your increased sensual awareness, I'll put you to the task with Sensual Experience exercises. For your special day or night of seduction, I've provided templates for you to create your very own Sensual Feast, no matter what your budget or dietary restrictions. I am a Master Sommelier, so you get the added bonus of expert wine pairing suggestions!

> *The Master Sommelier Diploma, granted by the UK-based Court of Master Sommeliers, is the ultimate professional credential that anyone can attain worldwide. The MS syllabus includes production methods of wines and spirits, international wine laws, harmony of food and wine, wine-tasting skills, and practical service and salesmanship, including service of liqueurs, brandies, ports, and cigars. In a*

blind tasting of six wines in twenty-five minutes, candidates must correctly identify grape varieties, country and region of origin, age, and quality. Hundreds begin but very few candidates successfully complete the program. 110 have earned the title, of which only 11 are women. Visit www.courtofmastersommeliers.org for more information.

I am a sensualist. I enjoy food. I make my living in wine, so I may pay more attention to sensual pleasures than others. My sensory receptors are no different than yours. They are simply more tuned in, for better and for worse. I make a conscious effort to employ them on a regular basis.

Just as in wine tasting, we use our senses, those of sight, smell, of taste, and occasionally of feeling, to enjoy food. Imagine putting a ripe, juicy piece of kiwi into your mouth and letting it sit there for a moment while your mouth and gums begin to tingle. Mmmm. Feel it.

Sight, smell, touch, and sound let us know how the food will taste. Even before you take a bite of tomato, your hands and nose will let you know if it's ripe.

—Margrit Biever Mondavi

I am obsessed with food. I roust myself out of bed in the morning following thoughts of what I will enjoy for breakfast. While working in the morning, I keep myself going with the thought of lunch. Later in the day, I fantasize about dinner. All throughout the day I'm thinking about the wine I'll enjoy with dinner and the glass that will help me drift off to sleep.

I fantasize about slipping naked into a vat of chocolate. Sometimes it's pudding, sometimes frosting, and on occasion it's a Jacuzzi full of frothy chocolate mousse. I see the picture of a 7-foot-tall champagne-glass whirlpool bath for two in a Poconos resort brochure and want to slide in. I wonder if they'd fill it with chocolate for me.

What is your fantasy? What will it take to unleash your wild sensual energy? Between these covers you'll find the answers. Make a little time to ignite a fire, to feel the heat, and to bask in the warmth of it.

I. Erotic Foods

1. Introduction

Welcome to *Erotic Foods*. In this guide we'll learn about erotic foods—their true aphrodisiac powers, their histories and origins, why they work, what will work best for you, and where to buy them. I'll also share tips on how to plan a Sensual Feast of your own, on any budget and for any taste (including one for vegetarians), and we'll have plenty of Sensual Experience exercises.

Rue de Babylone

Several years ago on an extended research mission in Paris, France, I was exposed to many new sensual pleasures. From my first bite of pain au chocolate to the sight of the Tour Eiffel, I was in heaven! It must have been fate that the maids' quarters I lived in were at the top of a building on the Rue de Babylone. Ancient Babylonians lived a luxurious, pleasure seeking, and occasionally immoral way of life.

What a Dish!

Cookie, tart, sweetie pie, dish, tall drink of water, and even "my little cabbage," or "mon petit chou," are words and phrases borrowed from the culinary world to refer to someone we are attracted to or in a relationship with.

2. Sensual vs. Sexual

Humans have been programmed over centuries to connect the word sensuality to sexuality. The very word "sensual" implies engaging the senses—of sight, of smell, of taste, of feeling, and of sound—warmly receiving and then focusing on the multitude of messages the physical being is experiencing. Senses nourish everything one does, from eating to napping, yet we have been made to feel guilty taking these idle pleasures; they are counterintuitive in a society and culture that is constantly on the go.

"Eroticism" is a focus on physical sensations that arouse sexual desire or bring sexual pleasure. Sensual experiences and pleasures may in fact arouse sexual desire, however they are not one and the same.

"Sensual" and "sensuous" are words defined by the *American Heritage Dictionary* as "pertaining to or derived from the senses, having qualities that appeal to the senses, readily susceptible through the senses; highly appreciative of the pleasures of sensation". Synonyms are "luxurious," "voluptuous," "sybaritic," and "epicurean."

3. Warm and Fuzzy

"Warm and fuzzy" is an undeniably good feeling. This good feeling is accessible to all. It is not reserved for certain individuals, nor is it limited to humans. Humans and other creatures are generally enabled to respond with sounds that reflect the sensations they are experiencing. The sounds give pleasure back to the pleasure provider, completing the circle in some master plan that is beyond our comprehension. Take, for example, the act of petting a cat. You stroke the cat; the cat feels warm and fuzzy. The cat purrs; you feel satisfied. The same circle of events is sometimes completed in lovemaking, and in the preparation of food. The cook relishes gathering each ingredient; he or she enjoys prepping, cooking, and presenting the dishes with flair. Though each step may require skill and concentration, it is a labor of love. For the dish to deliver pleasure, pleasure should go into its preparation. Pleasure, too, should go into its consumption, and it usually does. Sometimes we are just too stressed or harried to feel the full impact of the gift, leaving the pleasure giver without their well-earned reward.

Sensual Experience Exercise

Slowing down helps to focus your sensory receptors. Being hungry brings them into focus. When was the last time your mouth was watering, really watering, at the thought of what was to come? Allow yourself to feel hunger today.

grape goddess says:

Anticipation is a good first step towards maximizing sensual pleasure. Warm receptiveness is step two. Prepare to engage your sensorium, your entire sensory system.

The moment one gives close attention to anything, even a blade of grass, it becomes a mysterious, awesome, indescribably magnificent world in itself.

—Henry Miller

4. Slow Down

How does one enjoy food? Let me count the ways. Just as in wine tasting, one uses the senses, of sight, smell, and taste. Occasionally, the ears send pleasure messages. Pick up a flute of Champagne and listen to the self-renewing stream of bubbles. Tactile sense is also employed. Texture is a source of sheer sensual pleasure, especially when enhanced by positive jolts of flavor and aroma. Take caviar, for example. Those silky little globules slide across your palate, only to be squeezed softly and popped, their briny contents oozing out and coating your tongue. Perhaps you are not a fan of caviar. How about chocolate truffles? Just the sight of a truffle can bring a smile to the face of a chocolate lover.

Sensual Experience Exercise

Pick up a classic cocoa-dusted chocolate truffle and roll it gently between your fingers. Notice the dusting of cocoa powder on your fingertips, calling out for a cleansing lick. Don't lick, of course, until you have deposited the decadent morsel into your mouth. In it goes. Start to roll it around gently in your mouth. Feel the silkiness and taste the bitterness of the cocoa powder. Now bite into it, and enjoy that sweet, creamy, soft, and gooey core of chocolate. Is that bite the only thing you enjoyed? Look at each step, one by one. Each contributed to the total experience.

grape goddess says:

So often you're already reaching for the next truffle while biting into the first one. Only by slowing down and giving them your full attention can you take full advantage of the sensual pleasures they give.

5. Aphrodite, Goddess of Love and Beauty

Aphrodisiacs, nature's gift to humans and a way to keep the planet populated, are aptly named after Aphrodite, the Greek goddess of love, beauty, sexual ecstasy, and youth. Aphrodisiacs stimulate or intensify sexual desire, whether by their suggestive appearance, smell, flavor, texture, shape (for example, avocados are rich in flavor, smooth in texture, and shapely in form), or size, or by the nutrients, minerals, vitamins, or stimulants they provide for quick and efficient absorption into the body. The best aphrodisiacs are natural, and as fresh as possible. Categories include fruits and nuts, vegetables, spices and herbs, chocolate, coffee, fish, meat and eggs, cheese, honey, and wine.

When considering which aphrodisiacs to serve, keep in mind that males are visually stimulated (remember the joke about a man's dream date—opening the door to a naked woman holding a six-pack), while females are more often stimulated by a sense of comfort, well-being, and safety in pleasantly fragrant, soft, romantic surroundings. Pheromones (musky, sweaty aromas that emanate naturally from the body) are also erotic.

Sensual Experience Exercise

Go to the Body Shop, or any shop that sells fragranced oils, and ask for musk. Put your nose into the vial and inhale very softly, or use your hand to wave the aromas under your nose. Note your physical reaction, and also what comes to your mind immediately afterward.

The ultimate purpose of aphrodisiacs is to incite carnal love.

—Isabel Allende

6. Almonds, Figs, and the Mango

Almonds were a favorite of the Roman emperors. They have long been associated with passion and fertility. As a bonus, their consumption may slow the absorption of alcohol.

In ancient Greece, figs were one of the sacred foods associated with fertility and physical love. Figs, too, are considered aphrodisiacs in Italy, where it is said they resemble, when served flesh side showing, a highly erogenous zone of the female body.

grape goddess in the Jungle

Picking a ripe mango from a tree while riding bareback in the jungle of Costa Rica was an activity that stirred the most primal region of my being, the primal beast within. After biting into the tropical fruit, sweet, sticky juices rained down from my mouth onto my chest and begged for someone to come to the rescue and catch the drops. To my surprise, it was my horse's head that swung into action and licked the succulent nectar, arousing the opposite feelings of a sensuous encounter: shock and trepidation.

Just you and me, and a mango tree, the bare necessities of love.

—Michael Franks, "Bird of Paradise"

7. Dates, Coconut, and Acai

In *Aphrodite: A Memoir of the Senses*, Isabel Allende says, "The date provides energy and increases erotic potency in men and coquetry in women." Dates are rich in dietary fiber and potassium, are sodium, fat, and cholesterol free, and have an average of only twenty-four calories each. Robert Lower of Flying Disc Ranch in Thermal, California, also vouches for their aphrodisiac powers. In fact, his little vials of organic date pollen are a best-selling item. Oasis Date Gardens, also in Thermal, California, offers a full range of dates and date products, including one of my favorites, a 5-lb box of Choice Medjools.

Cleopatra bathed in coconut milk after a rubdown with coconut flakes before her assignations. Try organic virgin coconut oil from Tropical Traditions for the after-bath, pre-dinner rubdown. If you have a surplus of time and money, treat yourself and your partner to an Elemis exotic coconut rub and milk ritual wrap in the Mandara Spa on the Silversea fleet of small, super-luxurious cruise ships.

Acai, a small purple palm berry that grows wild in the Amazon and is imported to the U.S. by Sambazon, is said to give a natural rush. The proudly sensuous Brazilians enjoy Acai as a sort of sorbet, which is sold in big bowls by street vendors.

Aphrodisiacs are the bridge between gluttony and lust.

—Isabel Allende

8. Grapes, Quince, Apple, Pomegranate, and the Kiwi

In their natural state, grapes work well for seduction as they are easy to feed, slowly, one by one, to the seductee. Alternatively, you may choose to drape yourself languorously over the sofa and ask your potential lover to feed you, saying firmly while looking deeply and seductively into his or her eyes, "Peel me a grape." Select sweet, juicy, pit-free grapes. The quince, apple, and pomegranate are symbolic fruits of Aphrodite. A bowl of apples on the table is a nice, suggestive touch. Kiwi gives a tingly, numbing sensation to the tongue and gums.

Sensual Experience Exercise

Peel a ripe kiwi and slice into six discs. Set them on palate. Sit down side by side, and feed each other the fruit slices, licking each other's fingers if things are heating up. Talk for a moment or two, and then concentrate on the sensation you feel on your tongue and gums. Now, kiss each other.

No self-respecting orgy can do without grapes.

—Isabel Allende

9. Artichokes, Eggplant, Mushrooms, Garlic, Onions, and the Tomato

The pleasure Catherine de Medici took in consuming vast quantities of artichokes was considered scandalous at the time. The thorny green thistle buds were widely regarded as aphrodisiacs and were reserved for men only.

Earthy vegetables such as eggplant and mushrooms awaken natural instincts. Morel mushrooms or a sprinkle of porcini dust (from the bottom of a bag of dried porcinis) work wonders. Garlic raises red blood count and helps get the blood to the right places. In yogic nutritional philosophy, garlic and onions are *rajasic*, as are chocolate and coffee, and give heat to the body. Followers of this philosophy believe those who eat a diet high in *rajasic* substances may tend to be more aggressive, impatient, and opinionated. This is a small price to pay, I would say. I love the heat and all of its benefits. I am especially fond of garlic, and am constantly amazed by its aphrodisiacal powers.

Tomatoes, or the "love apples" thought to be Eve's temptation in the Garden of Eden, are known to keep male prostrate problems at bay. Notice a pattern here? These ingredients are the mainstays of the Mediterranean diet. Perhaps this is the reason for all the lovemaking there.

Sensual Experience Exercise

Arrange slices of eggplant, tomato, garlic and onion in a casserole dish. Lightly drizzle with olive oil, sprinkle with sea salt, and gently bake. Let cool. Serve to seductee. For a gold star, feed to seductee slowly, bite by savory bite.

The brief emergence of morels coincides with the season of rebirth and beauty, when nature springs awake with a sweeping mandate for all her subjects to breed. Seeking morels during this time puts lead in your pencil.

—John Ratzloff, food & wine writer

10. Fresh Truffles, Truffle Cream, Truffle Oil, and Truffle Juice

Truffles, a sort of underground mushroom, are precious, rare, and costly. Black or white, they are hunted, not gathered, and sell for up to $3000 per pound. Truffles awaken erotic and gastronomical dreams. Napoleon ate them before his clandestine meetings with Josephine. Isabel Allende says, "Scientists have discovered that the scent of the truffle activates a gland in the pig that produces the same pheromones present in humans when they are smitten by love. It is a sweaty, garlic-tinged odor that reminds me of the New York subway." Whatever works for you, baby.

Truffle oil is a relative bargain at two or three bucks per ounce considering how far a little goes. Pour lightly over a pizza, some pasta, or scrambled eggs. The scent alone may scramble the intellect. There is something deeply primitive and earthy in this aroma and flavor that awakens a raw, aggressive hunger deep within.

Truffle cream is a potent aphrodisiac. Mix into pasta and garnish with freshly-shaved pecorino, or melt half a teaspoon onto a steak.

Another option is to buy a small can of truffle jus/juice, such as the exquisite Etruria Gourmet Black Winter Truffle Juice, and add one-quarter teaspoon to one-half cup grapeseed oil. This is sex in a bottle; the unctuous, slippery texture of the oil blankets the tongue while the truffle flavor flames the innermost fires. Drizzle lightly on butter lettuce leaves that have been gently patted dry.

grape goddess says:

Imagine what would happen if one were offered truffle juice instead of orange juice each morning. No one would be able to get off to work!

If Adam and Eve did what they did for an apple, imagine what they would've done for a truffle-studded turkey.

—Jean Anthelme Brillat-Savarin

11. Heat Things Up—Spices and Herbs

Heat, whether from internal or external sources, stimulates nerve endings and relaxes muscles in the body. Cayenne and garlic help boost circulation, a natural for seduction. The tingling sensation of chili on the palate may lead to tingling sensations elsewhere. Super-sensitive types may prefer the milder flavors of cinnamon, fennel, and sweet onion. Freshly-ground peppercorns add heat. SeaStar sea salt, from a nature reserve in the Sea of Brittany, the cleanest sea in the world, is good to have on hand too. Pablo Neruda says of salt, "Dust of the sea, in you the tongue receives a kiss from ocean night." Yeah, baby. That gets the mojo going.

I like a raw egg served on my lover's navel, with chopped onion, salt, pepper, lemon, and a drop of Tabasco.

—Isabel Allende

Sensual Experience Exercise

Before your sensual feast, give yourself, or each other, a honey-salt rub so that your skin will be silky smooth and glistening.

12. Fruit of the Gods—Chocolate

Cocoa gives a sense of well-being and is said to be three times as effective as green tea in improving the health of males. Healthy specimens tap effortlessly into their vein of wild sensual energy, so keep the cocoa flowing. Cayenne-laced Spanish hot chocolate, a legendary elixir of love, and the cinnamon-, vanilla bean-, and almond-infused Mexican spiced cocoa (*Caffe d'Amore*) are two to try.

Theobroma, fruit of the gods, is the genus that includes the cacao tree. Cacao was the sacred drink of the Aztecs, consumed only by the nobility. Later, it came to be known as a powerful aphrodisiac by Spanish women. Allende says, "It is as addictive and stimulating as coffee—because of the alkaloid theobromine—but it is also symbolic in rituals of romantic courtship. What woman has seen her defenses crumble before a box of chocolates?"

Sensual Experience Exercise

Five Minutes and Fifty Cents:
Set an egg timer to five minutes. Sit down with your partner and one plain Hershey bar. Share it slowly, with the goal of making it last the entire five minutes.

One Hour and a Twenty:
Play the "Strip Chocolate" game (see shopping guide for details)

One Weekend and a Box Full of Benjamins:
Visit the Spa at Hotel Hershey, Pennsylvania, for a chocolate bath and more.

13. Café Olé

Coffee and tea stimulate the mind. If this your beverage of choice, select something with exotic, sensuous vanilla perfume, a tea noir such as Mariage Freres Vanille des Iles, or a full-bodied, gutsy, and seductive dark roast from Sumatra, such as Peet's Aged Sumatra. Coffee-producing islands in the Pacific have rich volcanic soil and tropical climates, giving full-bodied, rustic, and earthy flavors and aromas to their beans. Holding the mug will warm up cold hands, which is a very, very good thing for all parties.

Tip:

Be careful not to burn the kissing parts or to consume so much that you'll be running to the loo. This is not the kind of natural urge you want to pursue.

Sensual Experience Exercise

Visit your favorite coffee shop and go on a smell safari. Sniff several types of beans and several types of tea leaves. Take note of those that give you pause, and why. Purchase a little bit each of two or three types that turn you on, and try them out with a partner.

Good living is an act of intelligence, by which we choose things which have an agreeable taste rather than those which do not.

—Jean Anthelme Brillat-Savarin

14. Longing for a Kiss—Oysters and Fish

Powerful and swift, oysters are the most efficient of erotic foods. With their raw, briney, natural smell, a taste reminiscent of intimate body parts, and certainly a texture only the forces of nature uninterrupted could produce, oysters deliver on all counts. I celebrated a benchmark birthday recently. I figured that if I didn't try an oyster at this age, when would I ever? Like my experiences with garlic, the oysters jumpstarted my mojo, proving this one is not just for the boys. You go, girls!

Oysters, those seductive tears of the sea, which lend themselves to slipping from mouth to mouth like a prolonged kiss.

—Isabel Allende

The soft, seductive texture of sea bass works really well, too, though it is important not to overcook it. Also keep in mind that this fish can be pricey.

Abalone, clams, conch, scallops, shrimp, squid, and octopus also give good game. A cab driver I met in the Caribbean told me he and his wife had to give up conch after the birth of their eighth child!

Sushi may help get things started, but the downside is twofold. Dipping is tricky and often messy, and having to consume each piece whole smacks of gluttony, not seduction.

15. Lavish and Ravish—Caviar

A body needs nourishment and a spoonful of caviar works wonders as long as the target is not a caviar virgin. Often times the very song, painting, person, tie, drink, or food you dislike initially becomes your most highly prized friend. Caviar's fishiness, an early turn-off, eventually takes one out to a sea of bliss. Caviar's sleek and silky texture tantalizes the palate, while the occasional popping of the eggs flames the fires of primal awareness.

Petrossian and Caviarteria are two fine purveyors of caviar. Try pressed, or broken, caviar. Though not always available, it delivers everything but perfect round eggs and is significantly less costly.

grape goddess in Manhattan

I once booked the mink-upholstered booth at the Petrossian Restaurant in Manhattan for myself and a rather uninspired specimen as part of a research mission on male-female interpersonal relations. The sensations of caviar on my palate and fur on my thighs were sure to put me in the mood, if nothing else. Plus they served very, very good Champagne by the glass.

Food is created by the sex of plants or of animals; and we find it sexy.

—Diane Ackerman

16. What Are They Doing in There? Beef, Egg, and Game

On a recent research mission, I had a food orgasm with Argentinean beef. Freshly embarked on the *MS Silver Wind* and craving comfort food after a long flight and a bad meal in Rio, I ordered a cheeseburger to my cabin. One bite had me oohing, ahhing, and moaning so much that my new neighbors leaned over their balconies to see what was going on.

Italians give credit to raw meat in awakening their libidos, especially carpaccio, thin slices of raw beef dressed with olive oil, capers, and paper-thin shavings of parmigiano cheese. I met an Italian count on the *Silver Wind* who explained that his recipe for full power was four bananas and one *bistecca* (steak)!

Game birds, such as quail, are high on the aphrodisiac list. Utensils are tedious, so throw caution to the wind and use your fingers. The restorative power of eggs works wonders. They are quite useful when scrambled and used as a vehicle for truffle oil, or as a base for the frothy Italian dessert zabaglione, also known as "honeymoon sauce."

Buon Giorno, Bellissima!

In Italy, dressing, grooming, eating, drinking, driving, and lovemaking are arts to which many waking hours are devoted. I recommend Italy especially to females suffering from low self-esteem due to a dearth of flirtatious males in their 'hoods or to deficient boyfriends. Go over there and bask in the attention. Enjoy it for what it is!

17. Ace in the Hole—Cheese and Honey

While spray cheese does have a place in seduction—think location of application—the chemical taste doesn't tap into our primal nature. Cheese has PEA, or phenyl ethylamine, said to release the same hormone as sexual intercourse. Earthy, soft-textured cheeses work best, especially when served with a side of honeycomb or an eggcup of honey. Conveniently thick, sweet, gooey, and sticky, honey is the ace-in-the-hole of erotic foods. Try a creamy lavender-infused honey from Provence or a dark, mysterious chestnut honey from Italy. Fresh honeycomb is often found at farmer's markets and is available at the Oakville Grocery.

Sensual Experience Exercise

Apply honey to fingers, toes, and erogenous zones such as the underside of your partner's wrist, and then lick off slowly. Follow with a kiss.

My ace-in-the-hole cheese, especially when it is fully ripe and soft, is Red Hawk, from Cowgirl Creamery in Tomales Bay, California. Red Hawk is an artisanal (small-production, handcrafted) triple-cream, washed-rind, fully-flavored cheese made from organic cow's milk from the Straus Family Dairy. I also recommend Rochetta from Piedmont, Italy, or Sottocenere al Tartufo, from Venice, Italy. Both are softly textured cow's milk cheeses. Sottocenere al Tartufo is covered in an ash of nutmeg, cloves coriander, cinnamon, licorice, and fennel, is aromatized with truffle oil, and is studded with black truffles. Nibbling on this cheese sparks the inner flame. Fan the flames, and if things go well take little pieces and nibble from body parts that work as trays, such as the shoulder or, if horizontal, the neck. This is pure sensual pleasure magnified ten times over! Belgioioso Pepino is firm, nutty, and studded with black peppercorns, which pack a fiery little punch.

A dinner without cheese is like a beautiful woman with only one eye.

—Jean Anthelme Brillat-Savarin

18. Wine

Nectar of the gods, consolation of mortals, wine is a marvelous beverage that has the power to drive away worries and to give us, though it be for but an instant, a vision of Paradise. No one can argue the aphrodisiac power of wine: in moderate quantities it dilates the blood vessels, carrying more blood to the genitals and prolonging erection; it lessens inhibitions, relaxes, and fosters joy, three fundamental requirements for good performance, not only in bed but at the piano as well.

—Isabel Allende

Pinot Noir ("pee-no nwaahhr") is the number-one wine of seduction. The intoxicating, earthy scent of Pinot Noir brings even grape goddess to her knees. Instant arousal in a glass, tantalizing with its perfume and texture, Pinot Noir heightens and focuses sensual awareness like a camera zooming in for a close up on sheer sensual pleasure. I recommend Navarro Vineyards, Mendocino, Kenwood, Russian River Valley, Robert Mondavi Winery, Carneros, or Chambolle-Musigny Les Amoureuses, Burgundy, France. Champagne or sparkling wine is another excellent choice, though ultimately what will please your lover is what you should select.

It warms the blood, adds luster to the eyes, and wine and love have ever been allies.

—Ovid, *The Art of Love*

19. Now That's a Bubble Bath—Champagne

Ultra-feminine and lusciously curvaceous Marilyn Monroe once took a bath in 350 bottles of Champagne. Without Marilyn's bank account, but still curious, I took a bath in three, but I had to add warm water to fill up the tub. The tepid yellow bath water did nothing for me. A spontaneous Champagne shower is much more exciting, but seeing my man drinking Champagne from my shoe warms me to the very core.

Start a fire, rekindle it, or celebrate with the help of sparkling wine or Champagne. From California I recommend Korbel Chardonnay Champagne, Iron Horse Blanc de Blancs Sonoma County Green Valley, and Schramsberg Reserve. From France, try Domaine Laurens Blanquette de Limoux, Nicolas Feuillatte Blanc de Blancs Champagne, Bollinger Grand Année Brut Champagne, or Philipponnat Clos de Goisses Champagne.

Keeping the glasses lightly filled gives both of you frequent opportunities to get closer while topping up. Do nibble on olives such as kalamatas or lucques, nuts such as almonds or pistachios, and other light snacks while sipping. Wine consumed on an empty stomach is a no-no. With bubbly, this is even more important, as the CO_2 bubbles carry the alcohol immediately and directly into the bloodstream.

Sensual Experience Exercise

Set the stage with candlelight and soft music, open the bubbly, and serve two glasses, pouring in only enough to fill them halfway. Now, make a toast, looking deep into your partner's eyes. Before clinking glasses, intertwine arms, wrapping them around each other's until you are back in clinking position. Now, clink, and slowly unwrap, keeping direct eye contact the entire time. Once your arms are free, take a sip, and give each other a kiss.

Champagne with its foaming whirls, as white as Cleopatra's pearls.

—Byron

20. Sweet and Fortified Wine

Sweet wines are erotic elixirs when sipped out of a navel or from the nape of a neck—or, in more formal surroundings, sipped between bites of chocolate truffle torte. Bonny Doon Framboise, a raspberry-infused sweet wine, is good for population acceleration. For those who love oranges, I recommend Quady Essencia, a fortified American Orange Muscat dessert wine that is very reasonably priced.

Port is a popular and easy-to-find fortified sweet wine. A sip of sweet, raisin-imbued Tawny Port would serve well to sweeten the breath between kisses. Sip lightly and stop after one glass, or you may doze off and wake up with a brutal headache. Port hangovers are absolutely the worst!

Spirits, while they may lower inhibitions initially, end up deadening the senses and may even lower stamina.

I like to have a martini, two at the very most. After three I'm under the table, after four I'm under the host.

—Dorothy Parker

21. What Works for You?

To each their own. Your tastes and preferences are as unique as your fingerprints. Whether or not you dress a certain way or drive a certain car to give an impression or to fit in, what you eat and drink and how you make love will differ from just about anyone else out there. Relax, and go with your instincts. After all, getting in touch with your instincts is the first step towards maximizing sensual pleasures. The pleasure rainbow is a complimentary gift from nature. Now go out there and throw some game.

Sensual Experience Exercise

Highly coveted in centuries past, the maiden's thigh is still the center of attraction. In France, frogs' legs are known as *cuisses des nymphs*, or nymphs' thighs. It is said that the best Cuban cigars were rolled on the thighs of virgin maids. The ankle, a highly overlooked erogenous zone, is a delicious target. Imagine that you are with your partner and that things are going well. Imagine zoning in on the ankle. Start here and work your way, very slowly, up the leg.

22. What Works for Them?

Your tastes and preferences are unique, and you should embrace them. Keep in mind, though, that your partner will have unique tastes and preferences too. Your dreamy, decadent caviar may be "gross fish eggs" to someone else. To be most effective, do a little research. Ask little questions here and there in the weeks prior to the big event. Ask their friends and family members too for help.

Dress to impress, wearing fabrics that are soft to the touch, such as cashmere, lamb's wool, or silk. Don't overdo it with the fragrance. Keep aftershave, cologne, perfume, body fragrance, and hair products to a minimum. The aromas of erotic foods mixed with your own natural pheromones should do the trick.

Science has recently proved something that women, with far less study, have known for millennia: that amorous desire begins in the nose.

—Isabel Allende

23. Setting the Mood for Your Sensual Feast

Images of abandon and dissoluteness evoke sensuality, but sometimes, strangely, ritual and good manners can be exciting.

—Isabel Allende

Feel free to sit upright at a formal table and follow formal rules of etiquette if this puts you in your comfort zone. A Sensual Feast does work best, however, with the potential lovers sitting side by side on a loveseat or on a soft plush rug or blanket, with platters of food and drink set abundantly before them at arm's length. Seal the deal with soft lighting, if indoors, and with flowers, candlelight, and romantic music.

If a lady is involved, lay down a single rose, the premiere symbol of female sexuality, or a suggestive bowl of apples. Set within reach a few tendrils cut from fresh bulbs of fennel (anise) and use them to tickle the undersides of the wrists, elbows, knees, feet, the forehead, nose, lips, and nape of the neck.

Light a softly spicy or, better yet, fragrance-free candle. Avoid strong fruit or candied smells.

Have a selection of music on hand, from artists such as Chopin, Will Downing, Enya, Michael Franks, João Gilberto, Boney James, Al Jarreau, Norah Jones, Diana Krall, Luis Miguel, Vivaldi, and Barry White.

24. Hunting and Gathering for Your Sensual Feast

The pornographic experience is mechanical, fast, and scripted, whereas the erotic experience is slow, artistic, and completely unique. When selecting food and drink for your Sensual Feast, you'll want to taste the wild darkness of nature, not highly processed, preservative-filled, mass-produced, heavily-advertised industrial food.

Ripeness is all.

—William Shakespeare

Freshness is the goal, so start with the freshest possible ingredients. The aphrodisiac power of vegetables is in fact directly related to their freshness. Plan, shop, and prepare well in advance so you can concentrate on the sensual pleasures when the moment arrives. In a perfect world, you would make the rounds at a dozen or so specialty shops or at a farmer's market. If this is not possible, supplement your grocery store purchases with a few items ordered online. See chapter III for detailed shopping information.

If you have a Trader Joe's in your area, go there for low prices, especially for cheeses and condiments, including truffle oil, which they now carry seasonally. While a bit pricey, Whole Foods, Wild Oats, and other organic food stores are the best bets for your produce, meats, and fish. If price is no object whatsoever, visit Dean and Deluca. You are going to spend more than you might on a normal meal, but this is a special occasion, so start saving in advance. Think of this as an investment in your sensuality, but do not feel obligated to spend beyond your means. It is possible to seduce someone with a single bunch of grapes, or with a Hershey bar.

25. Sensual Feast $

$25–$40, plus wine

Appetizers:

Grapes
Toasted almonds, pistachios
Dolmathes (stuffed grape leaves)

Inglenook Chablis, California
Korbel Chardonnay Champagne, California
Domaine Laurens Blanquette de Limoux Brut nv, France

Main Course:

BBQ beef kabobs with onions and tomatoes

or

Grilled chicken and Japanese eggplant sautéed with garlic

Almaden Merlot, California
Hahn Syrah, Central Coast, California

Side Dish:

Macaroni and cheese drizzled with truffle oil
    Garnish with freshly-cracked peppercorns
    Keep the truffle oil handy for scrambled eggs the next morning (if things go well)

Dessert:

Fresh raspberries or candied orange slices in dark chocolate
    Dip fresh raspberries or candied orange slices in Hershey's Special Dark Chocolate Syrup
    Lick syrup off of the finger, inner wrist and forearm, thigh, and toe

or

Mango bread (see Recipe section)

Bonny Doon Framboise, California
Quady Essencia, California

Contrast is a primary principle throughout life from the moment of birth; light con-
trasts with dark, cold with warm, dry with wet, noise with silence, chaos with
rhythm. Balance in a meal is a studied achievement. Four rich courses at a banquet
infer long hours of gut-wrenching indigestion. On the other hand, contrasting highs
with lows, and rich with piquant, leaves a pleasant memory.

—Sid Goldstein

26. Sensual Feast $$

$40–$70, plus wine

Appetizers:

Grapes
Toasted almonds, pistachios
Truffle popcorn
    Lightly dust with sea salt and gently drizzle with truffle oil
Fennel pieces
    Serve pieces of breath-freshening fennel to each other between kisses

Woodbridge White Zinfandel, Sauvignon Blanc, or Viognier, California

Main Course:

Seared scallops with truffle oil
    Drizzle truffle oil over seared scallops just before serving

La Boatina Pinot Grigio, Friuli, Italy
Kenwood Pinot Noir Russian River Valley, California

or

Scampi André (see Recipe section)

Sacred Hills Whitecliff Sauvignon Blanc, New Zealand
La Boatina Pinot Grigio, Friuli, Italy

or

Grilled steak with truffle cream
    Melt half a teaspoon over grilled steak just before serving

Sokol-Blosser Meditrina, America
Amphora Winery Zinfandel, Dry Creek Valley, California
Benessere Sangiovese, Napa Valley, California

Side Dish:

Japanese eggplant sautéed with garlic

Cheese:

Belgioso Pepino cheese and honey
    Drizzle honey onto cheese (and other parts)
    Dip cheese (and other parts) into honey

Dessert:

Zabaglione ("Honeymoon sauce"—see Recipe section)
Chocolate truffles
    Purchase 2–4 in advance

Bonny Doon Framboise, California

I like restraint, if it doesn't go too far.

—Mae West

27. Sensual Feast $$$

$70–$180, plus wine

Appetizers:

Chilled oysters on the half-shell

or

Sevruga caviar with toast points and creme fraiche

Iron Horse Blanc de Blancs Sonoma County Green Valley, California
Nicolas Feuillatte Blanc de Blancs Champagne, France

First Course:

Scrambled eggs with truffle oil

or

Fresh black truffle sandwich
   Spread unsalted butter on soft rustic white bread. Add fresh black truffle shavings.

Hanzell Vineyards Chardonnay, Sonoma Valley, California
Corton-Charlemagne, Burgundy, France
(or continue with Champagne or sparkling wine)

Second Course:

Roasted quail with morels

Robert Mondavi Winery Pinot Noir, Carneros, Napa Valley, California
Chambolle-Musigny Les Amoureuses, Burgundy, France

or

Chilean sea bass with tangerine-serrano mojo (see Recipe section)

St. Supery Sauvignon Blanc, Napa Valley, California
Michel-Schlumberger Pinot Blanc, Dry Creek Valley, California

Third Course:

Lamb chops

or

Sirloin steak/filet mignon
    Serve plain, or prepare it with a peppercorn sauce as in Steak au Poivre

Clos du Val Merlot, Napa Valley, California
Dutton-Goldfield Syrah, Russian River Valley, California
Monsanto Chianti Classico Riserva, Tuscany, Italy
Villa Antinori, Tuscany, Italy

Side Dish:

Sautéed tomatoes, eggplant, and onions

or

Sautéed mushrooms

Cheese:

Cowgirl Creamery Red Hawk and honey comb or lavender honey
    Garnish with lavender buds

Dessert:

Vanilla bean ginger crème brulée
    Prepare or purchase in advance
    Garnish with violet flowers or violet candies

The Mariage Freres French Island Vanilla Black Tea, Paris
Navarro Vineyards Gewurztraminer Late Harvest Cluster Select, California

28. Sensual Feast Vegetarian

$35–$90, plus wine

Appetizers:

Medjool dates
Grapes
Toasted almonds, pistachios
Dolmathes (stuffed grape leaves)

Inglenook Chablis, California
Preston of Dry Creek Sauvignon Blanc, Dry Creek Valley, California
Bollinger Grand Année Brut, Champagne, France

Main Course:

Risotto with truffles and Champagne (see Recipe section)

or

Pasta with truffle cream and freshly-shaved pecorino

Bollinger Grand Année Brut, Champagne, France
Villa Antinori, Tuscany, Italy
Kenwood Pinot Noir Russian River Valley, California
Marimar Torres Pinot Noir, Russian River Valley, California

Side Dish:

Truffled butter lettuce salad (see Recipe section)

or

Heirloom tomato salad
    Slice tomatoes and drizzle with your best olive oil. Lightly dust with SeaStar sea salt.

Cheese:

Parmigiano Reggiano or pecorino and fresh figs

Garnish cheese with figs, flesh side showing, or a half a teaspoon of fig preserves

Dessert:

Mango slices
Chocolate truffles
    Purchase 2–4 in advance

Bonny Doon Framboise, California
Quady Essencia, California
Caffe d'Amore Mexican Spiced Cocoa

All cooks, like all great artists, must have an audience worth cooking for.

—André Simon, French gastronome

29. Nurture Nature

Why do we turn to nature for relaxation, for a sense of peace and well-being? Perhaps it is because being in a beautiful natural setting helps us to focus inward, to relax, to enjoy the sights, smells, and sounds, and to slow down. Nature's grand plan is something to consider. Engage your sensorium frequently and you'll be amazed at your newly found powers of both giving and receiving pleasure signals. You are a sensuous being. You have a physical connection with nature, art, food, and other creatures. Nourish that sensuous being. Feed it. Lavish it with affection. Let it grow! Then let it show!

I love watching a pair of red-tailed hawks dive, circle each other, and call out on a cool spring afternoon. I love surprising a bobcat in the vineyard in the early morning, and watching the antics of a slightly drunk coyote who ate too much freshly-pressed pomace.

—David Gates, VP vineyard operations, Ridge Vineyards, California

30. Congratulations

You've done it! You've unleashed your inner sensual self; you're in touch with the primal voice at the very core of your being. Who knew it would be so easy? After checking your progress with the following review quiz (for which you'll find the answer key on page 38), go out there with your big, goofy grin and enjoy *la dolce vita*, the good life. Sing in the shower, and sing in the streets!

If you'd like to brush up on your wine basics, check out *Wine*, part of the *grape goddess guides to good living* series. Visit www.planetgrape.com for details.

> *Gourmets capable of ordering from a French menu and discussing wines with the sommelier inspire respect in women, a respect that can easily be transmuted into a voracious, passionate hunger.*

—Isabel Allende

grape goddess says:

May the sensual pleasures of wine, food, and good living enrich your daily life and, on occasion, set your wild side free.

Check Your Success Quiz

1. Sensuality is

    a. engaging the senses.

    b. erotica.

    c. a focus on physical sensations that arouse sexual desire.

    d. the same as sexuality.

2. To focus your sensory receptors, you should

    a. eat a light meal.

    b. eat a rich meal.

    c. be hungry.

    d. take a shower.

3. Aphrodisiacs are

    a. effective only if taken on an empty stomach.

    b. only effective if suggestive in appearance or shape.

    c. most effective if derivative of animal protein.

    d. most effective if natural and fresh.

4. The pleasure Catherine de Medici took in consuming vast quantities of which item was considered scandalous at the time?

    a. morel mushrooms

    b. eggplant

    c. garlic

    d. artichokes

5. In yogic nutritional philosophy, garlic, onions, chocolate, and coffee are

    a. parts of a healthy, nutritious, balanced diet.

    b. *rajasic* and tend to promote more lovemaking.

    c. believed to cause aggressive, impatient, and opinioned behavior.

    d. healthy stimulants of digestion and blood circulation.

6. What secret ingredient unique to Spanish hot chocolate is said to induce wild, sensual energy?

    a. theobromine

    b. cayenne

    c. vanilla bean

    d. ground almonds

7. Which of the following is said to be three times as effective as green tea in improving the health of males?

    a. cocoa

    b. garlic

    c. salmon

    d. morel mushrooms

8. What is the fundamental aphrodisiac power of wine?

    a. silky texture

    b. erotic aromas and flavors

    c. dilation of blood vessels carrying more blood to the genitals

    d. aid to digestion so that the physical being can concentrate on love-making

9. The number-one wine of seduction is

   a. Champagne.

   b. Chardonnay.

   c. White Zinfandel.

   d. Pinot Noir.

10. When dressing for the big event, the key factor is

    a. wearing fabrics that are soft to the touch.

    b. wearing your most enticing cologne or perfume.

    c. dressing in tight, form-fitting clothing.

    d. keeping your hair in control with plenty of hair products.

Check Your Success Quiz Answer Key

1. a

2. c

3. d

4. d

5. c

6. b

7. a

8. c

9. d

10. a

II. Selected Recipes with Wine Pairings

Recipes: Sensual Feast $

Mango Bread

Preheat oven to 350°F.

2 c all-purpose flour
2 tsp cinnamon
2 tsp baking soda
1/2 tsp salt
1 1/2 c sugar
3 eggs, beaten
1 c salad oil
2 c mashed mangos
1/4 c walnuts
1 tsp vanilla

Sift together dry ingredients. Combine wet ingredients and fold into dry ingredients. Bake for 35 minutes or until soft to touch at center.

—Debbi Kenner, Honolulu, Hawaii

Wine Pairings for Mango Bread

Bonny Doon Framboise, California
Quady Essencia, California

Caffe d'Amore Mexican Spiced Cocoa

Recipes: Sensual Feast $$

Scampi André

Serves 4

20 shrimp (10/12 size)
1 bunch fresh sweet basil
3 oz Pernod
1 clove garlic (chopped fine)
3/4 pint whipping cream
All-purpose flour
salt and pepper
1 oz butter
1 oz oil

Clean and peel the shrimp, then remove the vein and cut the shrimp completely in half lengthwise. Season with salt and pepper and pass through flour lightly. Preheat frying pan with butter and oil at high heat. Sauté the shrimp fast so they brown slightly. Add garlic and very quickly discard all but 1 tbsp of the butter. Don't worry about losing some of the garlic. Mix in sweet basil and Pernod, and flambé (burn off the alcohol with a flame). Add the cream and stir until liquid concentrates slightly. Check seasoning. Serve immediately.

—Recipe provided by Andre Rochat, chef and proprietor of André's French Restaurant of Las Vegas.

Wine Pairings for Scampi André

Sacred Hills Whitecliff Sauvignon Blanc, New Zealand
La Boatina Pinot Grigio, Friuli, Italy

Recipes: Sensual Feast $$

Zabaglione ("Honeymoon Sauce")

Serves 2

3 large egg yolks
3 tbsp sugar
3 tbsp dry Marsala
Strawberries or raspberries (optional)

In a medium saucepan, or the bottom half of a double-boiler, bring about 2 inches of water to a simmer.

In a heatproof bowl that fits comfortably over the saucepan, or in the top half of the double boiler, beat the egg yolks, sugar, and Marsala with a hand-held electric mixer or whisk until well blended. Place over the simmering water—do not allow the water to boil. Beat the egg mixture until it is pale yellow and very fluffy, 3 to 5 minutes. Serve immediately, with fresh berries, if desired.

—Recipe by Michele Scicolone, *Sopranos Family Cookbook.*

Wine Pairing for Zabaglione

Bonny Doon Framboise, California

Recipes: Sensual Feast $$$

Chilean Sea Bass with Tangerine-Serrano Mojo

Serves 6

12 tangerines or 1 small can of tangerine sections in natural juice
2 serrano chiles, finely chopped
4 shallots, finely minced
3 tbsp finely chopped chives
1 roasted red bell pepper, peeled, seeded and sliced lengthwise into ¼-inch-thick pieces
1/4 c freshly-squeezed lime juice
1/4 c lemon oil
1 tbsp chopped parsley
1 tbsp chopped cilantro
6 Chilean sea bass fillets, 6-ounces each
2 tbsp oil
Kosher salt and freshly-ground black pepper

To prepare the mojo, extract the juice from 10 of the tangerines, then strain into a small saucepan. Gently reduce the liquid by half to concentrate the tangerine flavor. Place the reduced juice in a bowl to cool.

With a sharp paring knife, cut away the rind of the 2 remaining tangerines to expose the pulp, then cut between the segments alongside the thin membrane to remove the segments. Discard any seeds and add the tangerine segments to the bowl of juice. Add the chiles, shallots, chives, lime juice, lemon oil, parsley, and cilantro.

Mix well and set aside.

Brush the fish with oil and season with salt and pepper. Grill over medium heat. When it is done, spread the red bell pepper in the middle of the serving plate. Place the fish on top of the peppers and pour a 2-oz ladle of mojo sauce over the fish.

—Recipe provided by Andre Rochat, chef and proprietor of André's French Restaurant of Las Vegas.

Wine Pairings for Chilean Sea Bass with Tangerine-Serrano Mojo

St. Supery Sauvignon Blanc, Napa Valley, California
Michel-Schlumberger Pinot Blanc, Dry Creek Valley, California

Recipes: Sensual Feast Vegetarian

Risotto with Truffles and Champagne

Serves 2

2 c beef broth (mushroom broth may be substituted)
3 c water
3 tbsp unsalted butter
1 tbsp olive oil
¼ c minced shallots or onion
1 c medium-grain rice, such as Arborio or Carnaroli
½ c Champagne or dry white wine
Salt and freshly-ground pepper
1 fresh white or black truffle, or use a jarred truffle

In a saucepan, combine the broth and water, bring to a simmer, and keep warm over very low heat.

In a deep, wide saucepan or skillet, melt 2 tablespoons of the butter with the oil over medium heat. Add the shallots and cook for 5 minutes, or until softened but not browned.

Add the rice and stir for 1 minute. Add the Champagne and cook, stirring until most of the liquid is absorbed. Add ½ cup of the broth and cook, stirring until the liquid is absorbed. Continue cooking, adding the broth ½ cup at a time and stirring until it is absorbed, for 18 to 20 minutes, or until the rice is *al dente*, tender yet firm to the bite. If you are using jarred truffle, add the liquid from the jar to the rice. About halfway through the cooking time, add salt and pepper to taste. The rice should be moist and creamy. Add more liquid if necessary; if you run out of broth, use water.

If using a fresh truffle, spoon onto plates, then with a truffle shaver or vegetable peeler, shave the truffle over the risotto. If using a jarred truffle, chop it finely and stir it into the risotto. Stir in the remaining 1 tablespoon butter. Serve immediately.

—Recipe by Michele Scicolone, *Sopranos Family Cookbook*

Wine Pairings for Risotto with Truffles and Champagne

Bollinger Grand Année Brut, Champagne, France
Villa Antinori, Tuscany, Italy
Kenwood Pinot Noir, Russian River Valley, California
Marimar Torres Pinot Noir, Russian River Valley, California

Recipes: Sensual Feast Vegetarian

Truffled Butter Lettuce Salad

Buy a small can of truffle jus/juice, such as the exquisite Etruria Gourmet Black Winter Truffle Juice, and add ¼ teaspoon to ½ cup grapeseed oil. Drizzle lightly on butter lettuce leaves that have been gently patted dry.

—Recipe created by the Author

III. grape goddess Recommends

Aphrodisiacs to Eat

Organic Date Pollen
Flying Disc Ranch, Thermal, California
(760) 399-5313, Robert Lower

Choice Medjool Dates
Oasis Date Gardens, Thermal, California
(800) 827-8017
www.oasisdategardens.com.

Dolmathes (stuffed grape leaves)
Mediterranean markets or www.oakvillegrocery.com

Truffle Oil
Etruria Organically Grown Black, or White Truffle Oil
www.etruriagourmet.com

Truffle Jus/Juice
Etruria Gourmet Black Winter Truffle Juice
www.etruriagourmet.com or www.deandeluca.com ($68 for a 14 oz can)

Black Truffle Cream ($24 for 2.8 oz)
www.deandeluca.com

White Truffle Cream ($38 for 2.8 oz)
www.deandeluca.com

Sea Salt
SeaStar Sea Salt

(707) 942-9494
www.seastarseasalt.com

Caviar
Petrossian
(800) 828-9241
www.petrossian.com
Petrossian shops/restaurants in Manhattan, Los Angeles, Las Vegas, and Paris or select Nieman Marcus stores

Caviarteria
(800) 4-Caviar
www.caviarteria.com
Caviarteria shops in Manhattan, Beverly Hills, Las Vegas, and South Beach

Fresh Honeycomb
www.oakvillegrocery.com

Soft Textured Cow's Milk Cheeses

    Red Hawk Cheese
    Cowgirl Creamery, Tomales Bay, California
    (415) 663-9335
    www.cowgirlcreamery.com

    Rochetta from Piedmont, Italy
    Available at fine cheese shops nationwide

    Sottocenere al Tartufo, from Venice, Italy
    Available at fine cheese shops nationwide

Belgioso Pepino Cheese
www.belgioso.com

Hershey's Special Dark Chocolate Syrup
Grocery and specialty shops

Aphrodisiacs to Drink

Coffee, Tea, and Cocoa

Seductive Coffee
Peet's Aged Sumatra
Peet's shops
www.peets.com ($14.00 for 1 lb)

Exotic Tea
Mariage Freres Vanille des Iles
www.mariagefreres.com or www.williams-sonoma.com ($14.00 for a 3.5 oz tin)

Spiced and Flavored Hot Chocolate
Caffe d'Amore
(800) 999-0171
www.caffedamore.com

Wine
All wines are listed with approximate retail prices. If you have trouble finding a wine, visit www.wine-searcher.com or send an email to grapegoddess@ planetgrape.com.

Champagne and Sparkling Wine

Korbel Chardonnay Champagne, California, $11

Iron Horse Blanc de Blancs Sonoma County Green Valley, California, $28

Schramsberg Reserve, California, $65

Domaine Laurens Blanquette de Limoux, France, $14

Nicolas Feuillatte Blanc de Blancs, Champagne, France $45

Bollinger Grand Année Brut, Champagne, France, $90

Philipponnat Clos de Goisses Champagne, France, $130

White Wine

Inglenook Chablis, California, $6 for 1.5 L (Colombard sweetened with Muscat)

Woodbridge White Zinfandel, Sauvignon Blanc, or Viognier, California, $10

Michel-Schlumberger Pinot Blanc, Dry Creek Valley, California, $21

La Boatina Pinot Grigio, Friuli, Italy, $14

Sacred Hills Whitecliff Sauvignon Blanc, New Zealand, $16

Preston of Dry Creek Sauvignon Blanc, Dry Creek Valley, California, $16

St. Supery Sauvignon Blanc, Napa Valley, California, $17

Hanzell Vineyards Chardonnay, Sonoma Valley, California, $35

Corton-Charlemagne, Burgundy, France, $60–$90 (Chardonnay)

Red Wine

Navarro Vineyards Pinot Noir, Mendocino, California, $15
(Winery direct only, www.navarrovineyards.com)

Kenwood Pinot Noir, Russian River Valley, California, $17

Marimar Torres Pinot Noir, Russian River Valley, California, $32

Robert Mondavi Winery Pinot Noir, Carneros, Napa Valley, California, $35

Chambolle-Musigny Les Amoureuses, Burgundy, France, $40–$80 (Pinot Noir)

Hahn Syrah, Central Coast, California, $12

Dutton-Goldfield Syrah, Russian River Valley, California, $35

Sokol-Blosser Meditrina, America, $18 (Syrah/Pinot Noir/Zinfandel blend)

Amphora Winery Zinfandel, Dry Creek Valley, California, $24

Benessere Sangiovese, Napa Valley, California, $26

Monsanto Chianti Classico Riserva, Tuscany, Italy, $18 (Sangiovese)

Villa Antinori, Tuscany, Italy, $22 (Sangiovese blend)

Almaden Merlot, California, $6 for 1.5 L

Clos du Val Merlot, Napa Valley, California, $20

Sweet Wine—Raspberry Flavored
Bonny Doon Framboise, California, $11 (375 ml)

Sweet Wine—Orange Flavored
Quady Essencia, California, $15.50

Sweet Wine—Spicy
Navarro Vineyards Gewurztraminer Late Harvest Cluster Select, California, $25
(375ml)
(Winery direct only, www.navarrovineyards.com)

Erotic Body Products and Spas

Musk Oil
The Body Shop
www.thebodyshop.com

Organic Virgin Coconut Oil
Tropical Traditions
www.tropicaltraditions.com

Chocolate Spa
Spa at Hotel Hershey, Pennsylvania, USA
www.hersheypa.com/accommodations/the_spa_at_hotel_hershey/

Elemis Exotic Coconut Rub & Milk Ritual Wrap
Mandara Spa, at Sea
MS Silver Wind
www.silversea.com

Erotic Cruise

MS *Silver Wind*
www.silversea.com

Erotic Game

Strip Chocolate Game
Available at Target stores ($19.95)
www.target.com

Sensual Feast Music

Chopin
Will Downing
Enya
Michael Franks
João Gilberto
Boney James
Al Jarreau
Norah Jones
Diana Krall
Luis Miguel
Vivaldi
Barry White

IV. Sensual Experience Exercise Notebook

Write down your sensual experiences, including date, locations, and partners. This will make great reading later on!

_____
_____
_____
_____
_____
_____
_____
_____
_____
_____
_____
_____
_____
_____
_____
_____
_____
_____
_____
_____
_____
_____
_____
_____
_____
_____
_____
_____
_____

V. Bibliography

Ackerman, Diane. *A Natural History of the Senses.* New York: Random House, 1990.

Allende, Isabel. *Aphrodite: A Memoir of the Senses.* New York: HarperCollins Publishers, 1998.

Brillat-Savarin, Jean Anthelme. *The Physiology of Taste, or Meditations on Transcendental Gastronomy.* Translated by M. F. K. Fisher. Washington, D.C.: Counterpoint, 1949.

Franks, Michael. *Abandoned Garden.* New York: Warner Bros. Records Inc., a Time Warner Company, 1995.

Gates, David. *Ridge Vineyards Newsletter.* Santa Cruz: Ridge Vineyards, 2004.

Goldstein, Sid. *The Wine Lover's Cookbook.* San Francisco: Chronicle Books. 1999.

Griffin, Susan. *The Book of the Courtesans: A Catalog of Their Virtues.* New York: Broadway Books, 2001.

Mondavi, Margrit Biever, with Robert Mondavi and Carolyn Dille. *Seasons of the Vineyard.* New York: Simon and Schuster, 1996.

Morris, William, ed. *American Heritage Dictionary.* Boston: Houghton Mifflin Company, 1978.

Rucker, Allen, compiled by Artie Rucco, with recipes by Michele Scicolone. *Sopranos Family Cookbook.* New York: Warner Books, 2002.

VI. About the Author

Meet grape goddess

Catherine Fallis is the fifth woman in the world to have earned the title of Master Sommelier. In 1997, the UK-based International Court of Master Sommeliers granted her this prestigious designation, making her one of only eleven female MSs in the world. She holds a Bachelors of Science degree from Cornell University's School of Hotel Administration.

Fallis is founder and president of planet grape, a company committed to bringing a passion for wine, food, and good living into the lives of everyday people. She is creator of the *grape goddess guides to good living*, a range of lifestyle books, seminars, and e-learning programs on wine, food, and travel, including *Wine, Champagne & Sparkling Wine, Erotic Foods*, and *Cruising*.

She is also a guest host on NBC-11 TV's *In Wine Country*, director of education for VinoVenue, and an instructor at the Culinary Institute of America, Greystone. She was introduced to wine while backpacking around Europe in her college days and honed her skills later when she returned to live in Florence and Paris. Upon her return to New York, she continued her education of wine and food in five-star houses, working with industry luminaries Alain Sailhac at Le Cirque, Leona Helmsley at the Helmsley Palace Hotel, and Kevin Zraly at Windows on the World. In 1993, she joined the harvest team with Jean-Michel Cazes and Daniel Llose at Chateaux Pichon-Baron and Lynch-Bages, in Bordeaux, France.

Since then she has designed wine programs for some of the most celebrated restaurants and resorts in the United States, including Aqua, Pebble Beach Resorts, and the Beverly Hills Hotel, and at sea for luxury liners like the *Queen Elizabeth 2* and the *Yachts of Seabourn*. She worked as wine manager for a distributor, Paradise Beverages, in Honolulu, as district manager for a supplier, Seagram Classics, covering Greater Los Angeles, and as chief retail wine buyer at Beltramo's, in Menlo Park, giving her a unique, multi-faceted perspective on the wine industry.

In addition to writing wine columns for the *San Francisco Chronicle, San Francisco Examiner, Touring and Tasting, Santé,* and numerous other publications, she is chief consulting editor for *The Encyclopedic Atlas of Wine* (Global Publishing), editor of the *Pocket Encyclopedia of Wine* (Portable Press/Advantage Publishers), has penned chapters in *The Global Encyclopedia of Wine* (Wine Appreciation Guild), *The Chalk Hill Winery Sommelier Guide to Restaurants in America* (Chalk Hill Press), *America: The Complete Story* (Global Publishing), and *Travelers' Tales.* She worked on vineyard mapping for Oz Clarke's *Wine Atlas* (Little, Brown and Company), co-edited the Beverage Testing Institute's *Guide to Buying Wine* series, and published their premiere issue of *Tastings, The Journal.*

Catherine gives frequent educational presentations to consumers and to the trade, and she volunteers her time to charitable events. She is a mentor and role model for many young men and women entering the industry, is a member of numerous wine societies, and is frequently asked to lend her palate as a wine judge. She has financially supported three foster daughters through the Childreach organization and is working towards becoming a certified foster parent. In her free time she enjoys hiking in the mountains, horseback riding, skiing, sea kayaking, and sabering champagne. A novice gardener, she is wondering how to cultivate white truffles in her backyard.

From Another Planet

For pretty much as long as I can remember, my friends and colleagues have commented that I came from another planet, so I figured I may as well call my business planet grape and create a cartoon character as my alter ego to boot! Who is grape goddess? She is the cartoon character I created to bring wine, food, and good living into the lives of people just like you.

grape goddess, Fearless Leader of planet grape

- mission statement: Bringing wine, food, and good living down to Earth

- what I do: educate Earthlings with my *grape goddess guides to good living* programs, an integral component of the *grape goddess guides to good living* media platform encompassing Internet, print, broadcast, and consumer-direct outlets

- visit planet Earth frequently, traveling on interplanetary shuttles

- able to assume human form so as not to intimidate Earthlings

- monitor Earthling activities from my Intergalactic Observation Station

- offer intergalactic customer empowerment and service from my support staff on planet Earth, the Wine Police and the Snob Squad

- *Don't make me send out the Wine Police!*

- *Don't make me send out the Snob Squad!*

grape goddess didn't fall from a shooting star:

> Wine was never a part of my life growing up on planet grape. The procreators weren't often around. Luckily, the other offspring and I had plenty of company—popular American television shows that came beaming in from the Intergalactic Observation Station—and interplanetary shuttles to planet Earth brought lots of contact with American culture. So it was that I grew up on an Earthling diet of Kool Aid, mac 'n cheese, Pringles potato chips, and Ho Ho's, enjoyed with the other offspring while watching *I Love Lucy* and *Star Trek.*
>
> Growing up in some pretty rough hoods, I always thought, there's gotta be something better than this. I started working at age twelve, and, finally, by my college days, had saved enough money to take an interplanetary shuttle to planet Earth, and headed for Europe. To stretch my funds, I took overnight train rides, sleeping on the luggage racks above the seats. Bread and cheese, and, to my delight, wine, were dietary staples for even those of modest means. For the first time, I saw that wine was an integral component of the meal, rather than a cocktail, and that dining was a joyful, communal, sensually charged, and satisfying experience. From that moment, I recognized my life's calling.

Dear grape goddess

"Thank you for everything you are doing for wine. God Bless You."
Robert Mondavi, Napa Valley

You have a special gift to teach and both Vida and I learned soooooo much!!!"
Robert and Vida Clay, Charleston, South Carolina

"Catherine gave me the confidence to not feel I have to agree with all the US wine magazine reviews for "big" wines, that character, personality, and complexity count."
Skay Davidson, Massage Therapist, Berkeley, California

"The energy with which you devote yourself to your work is inspiring, and so is all of the creativity that comes pouring out of you. Your writing is highly descriptive and evocative."
Paul Kaihla, Senior Writer, *Business 2.0—Time Warner*

"Thanks to grape goddess, I am no longer intimidated when I go to the liquor store by the "wall of wines" or confused when I am handed a wine selection menu at a restaurant!"
Erin Reynolds, 26 yrs old, Chicago

"Your wine pairings were the best I've had in my life!"
Robert Redford, at Aqua Restaurant, San Francisco, June 20, 2003

"Catherine, the grape goddess, encouraged me to be open and receptive to new aromas and tastes—a terrific way to learn about geography and culture."
John Nutt, Berkeley, California

"A great performance! Thank you for your expertise at Richie's 41st birthday!"
Heather Locklear, Los Angeles, California, July 11, 2001

"You are this unusual combination of quirky and refined. I loved your Champagne presentation and sabering at the Bubble Lounge!"
Marlene Anthony, Travel Specialist, San Francisco, February 18, 2004

"Wow is all I can say-such a dramatic and showy presentation! Everyone loved watching your sabering! Thank you for sharing your passion with our guests."
Stephanie Harkness, Silicon Valley Capital Club, November 1, 2003

"Your demonstration was terrific. You really know how to "wow" the crowd."
Carissa Chappellet, Chappellet Vineyard, Napa Valley, November 7, 2003

Catherine shows no preference for California but is familiar with wines from every continent."
***Uit-magazine*, Belgium**

"Catherine is intelligent, very attractive, has a quick wit, and possesses great intrigue."
Wilfred Wong, e-Commerce Cellarmaster, Beverages and More, Concord, California

"The way you explain things makes me want to learn more."
Kathy Mintun, Bartender, Aqua Restaurant

"Thank you for all your expertise and insights You vastly improved my passion, knowledge and professionalism."
Rodney Schick, Aqua Restaurant, San Francisco

"Catherine,
I came away from the Sommelier Summit with so many awesome experiences, but one of the ones I will carry with me the longest is listening to your words of encouragement in the back of that sweaty little plane to Paso Robles. I came home more fired up than ever to sit for my next level of tests. Thank you very much."
John Paddon, Sommelier, Commander's Palace, New Orleans

"We are so fortunate to have women like you who have forged the way into the male-dominated world of advanced wine education."
Patti Hogan, Sommelier-at-large, Seattle

"I have known Catherine for fifteen years. She was my assistant at Windows on the World. She has a great personality, has great presentation, has great ability to work with a variety of people, and does it gracefully. I have a tremendous amount of respect for her."
Kevin Zraly, president of Wine Services International, New Paltz, NY

"The power of Catherine Fallis lies in her wine tasting palate—so sharp, so precise!—and as we all know in the business, the key to a strong palate is ability to communicate. Words come as easily from Catherine Fallis as honey from the bee. There are a lot of brilliant wine professionals serving in the industry today, but few come as worldly and well spoken as Catherine. Obviously, I am one of her biggest and longtime (over 10 years) fans. But as far as I know, everyone who has worked with her, or for whom she has done work, feels the same!"
Randal Caparoso, Founding Partner, Roy's Restaurant, Winemaker, and Writer

You give people faith and courage to move forward."
Lars Ryssdal, Fine Wine Manager, Young's Columbia Distributing, Seattle

"I get two or three calls a day about Catherine. She is just so approachable."
Michael Mina, Former Chef and Partner, Aqua Development Corporation, San Francisco, March 20, 2002

"Your work, image, presence and visibility have helped and inspired me so much. Thank you."
Jean Arnold-Sessions, CEO, Hanzell Vineyards, Sonoma, October 16, 2003

"You are the best."
Steven Olson aka The Wine Geek

Catherine Fallis, MS
Planet Grape LLC
240 Lombard Street, #826
San Francisco, California, 94111
(415) 834-0784
(415) 425-5828
grapegoddess@planetgrape.com

0-595-32698-6

Printed in the United States
24870LVS00001B/670-849

9 780595 326983